Jaguars

by Darlene R. Stille

Content Advisers: Terrence E. Young Jr., M.Ed., M.L.S.,
Jefferson Parish (La.) Public Schools, and Janann Jenner, Ph.D.

Reading Adviser: Dr. Linda D. Labbo,
Department of Reading Education, College of Education,
The University of Georgia

COMPASS POINT BOOKS

Minneapolis, Minnesota

FIRST REPORTS

Compass Point Books
3722 West 50th Street, #115
Minneapolis, MN 55410

Visit Compass Point Books on the Internet at *www.compasspointbooks.com* or e-mail your request
to *custserv@compasspointbooks.com*

Photographs ©: John Guistina/FPG International, cover; Lynn M. Stone, 4; Planet Earth
Pictures/FPG International, 5; Photo Network/Mark Newman, 7; Kjell B. SandvedVisuals
Unlimited, 8; Mark Newman/Tom Stack & Associates, 9; Mundy Hackett/Visuals Unlimited, 10;
Frederick D. Atwood, 11, 29, 34; Tom Brakefield/Corbis, 12–13, 18; Tom and Pat Leeson, 14; W.
Perry Conway/Tom Stack and Associates, 16; Unicorn Stock Photos/Robert E. Barber, 17; Eda
Rogers, 19; Brian Parker/Tom Stack and Associates, 20; A. Schmidecker/FPG International, 22,
24; Richard Day/Daybreak Imagery, 23; David L. Brown/Tom Stack and Associates, 27, 28;
Unicorn Stock Photos/Robert Ginn, 30; Archive Photos, 31; Pat Anderson/Visuals Unlimited,
32–33; Joe McDonald/Visuals Unlimited, 35, 40–41; Hulton-Deutsch Collection/Corbis, 36–37;
Kevin Schafer/Corbis, 38–39; Lynn M. Stone, 42; XNR Productions, Inc., 46.

Editors: E. Russell Primm, Emily J. Dolbear, and Melissa Stewart
Photo Researcher: Svetlana Zhurkina
Photo Selector: Linda S. Koutris
Designer: Bradfordesign, Inc.

Library of Congress Cataloging-in-Publication Data
Stille, Darlene R.
    Jaguars / by Darlene Stille.
      p. cm. — (First reports)
    Includes bibliographical references and index.
    ISBN 0-7565-0055-9 (hardcover : lib. bdg.)
    1. Jaguar—Juvenile literature. [1. Jaguar. 2. Endangered species.] I. Title. II. Series.
    QL737.C23 S75 2001
    599.75'5—dc21   00-010912

Table of Contents

Meet the Jaguar

▲ *A jaguar resting in the shade*

It is early evening in the rain forest. The trees block the last rays of the sun. The path along the riverbank is dark. Everything is silent.

A pair of yellow eyes glows in the thick leaves. The eyes watch a turtle crawl along the riverbank. Suddenly, the branches spring open. A big cat leaps onto the tur-tle. It clamps the turtle in powerful jaws. The turtle's

▲ *A jaguar looks for food in the river.*

5

shell breaks with a loud crack. The turtle is the big cat's dinner.

The cat is a jaguar. The jaguar is the largest and most powerful of the wild cats living in Central and South America.

The name *jaguar* comes from a word used by South American Indians to describe the animal. The name means "a beast that kills its **prey** with one bound." Animals hunted for food by other animals are called prey.

What Do Jaguars Look Like?

A jaguar's fur may be gold, tan, or black. The fur under the animal's chin and on its belly is white.

All jaguars have spots. Some of the spots are shaped like large rings with small dark spots inside them. The spots on the jaguar's back sometimes look like stripes. Jaguars look like leopards but they are larger.

An old Indian story tells how the jaguar got its spots. In the

▲ *Jaguars have beautiful fur.*

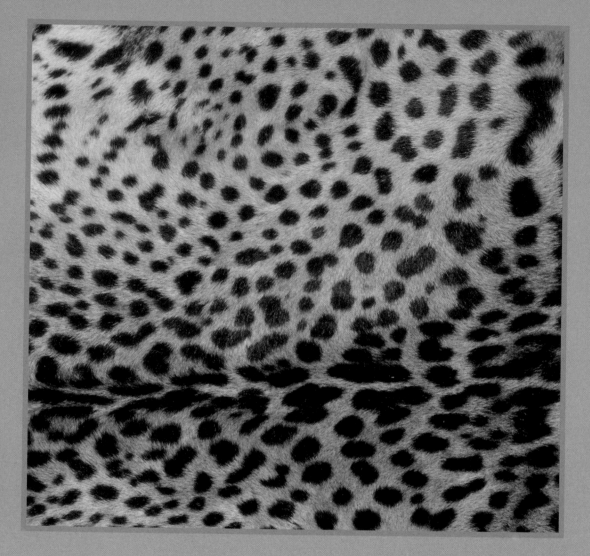

story, the jaguar made the spots on its fur with its
muddy paws. This is not a true story, of course—but
a jaguar's spots look very much like paw prints!

A jaguar's body ripples with powerful muscles. Its legs are short and sturdy and its head is wide. The jaws of a jaguar are square. They are strong enough to bite through bone.

▲ *Jaguars have strong, square jaws.*

▲ *The only cats bigger than jaguars are tigers (above) and lions (opposite).*

The jaguar makes fierce and loud sounds. Sometimes a jaguar snarls. Sometimes it growls, grunts, or roars. The jaguar is one of the four roaring cats. The other roaring cats are the leopard, lion, and tiger. These cats roar to let other animals know that they are nearby.

Jaguars are very big cats. Only the lions of Africa and tigers of Asia are bigger cats than jaguars. The jaguars in South America are the largest kinds of jaguars.

▲ *Male jaguars (left) are bigger than the females (right)*

Male jaguars weigh 125 to 250 pounds (57 to 114 kilograms). Some male jaguars weigh as much as 350 pounds (159 kilograms). Female jaguars weigh about 100 to 200 pounds (45 to 90 kilograms).

Jaguars may be 4 to 6 feet (1.2 to 1.8 meters) long—not including their tails! Their tails are 18 to 30 inches (46 to 76 centimeters) long.

Jaguars are not very tall. They have short legs. Their shoulders are only about 2 feet (60 centimeters) above the ground.

Where Do Jaguars Live?

▲ *This jaguar lives in the rain forests of Central America.*

Jaguars live in parts of Mexico, Central America, and South America. Most jaguars live in rain forests and wet grasslands. But some live in dry forests.

Jaguars live where there are trees, tall grasses, or bushes. They are good at climbing trees. They often live near lakes, rivers, or streams. Jaguars love water. They are excellent swimmers too.

▲ *Jaguars are good swimmers.*

▲ *The jaguar's coat colors help it blend into its background.*

An animal's fur is called its **coat**. The color of a jaguar's coat depends on where the animal lives. Its color helps the animal blend in with its surroundings. Then it can hide when it is hunting food.

For example, jaguars that live in open, grassy places have light coats. Jaguars that live in dark forests have dark coats. The dark-colored jaguars that live in the Amazon rain forest of Brazil are called black jaguars.

▲ *A young black jaguar*

What Do Jaguars Eat?

▲ *A wild jaguar attacks a peccary.*

Jaguars eat other animals. Jaguars hunt more than eighty different kinds of prey. They hunt monkeys, turtles, armadillos, deer, frogs, fish, wild pigs, and peccaries. Peccaries are related to pigs. Jaguars even hunt animals called **caimans**. Caimans are one type of alligator.

Jaguars hunt at night as well as in the daytime. They always hunt alone. Sometimes they walk along a road or a trail looking for prey. Often, they hide in tall grasses or bushes, waiting for an animal to pass by.

▲ *A jaguar waits in tall grass for its prey.*

▲ Jaguars are powerful cats.

These big cats often walk through the water in rivers and streams to catch fish and frogs. They can catch large prey, such as deer, with their powerful jaws. They kill the animal by crushing its skull with their teeth.

Jaguars use their paws to kill smaller prey. One swipe of a jaguar's paw will kill a dog or a **rodent**. A rodent is a small animal that nibbles, such as a squirrel or a mouse.

Jaguars do not have to worry about larger animals stealing their prey. No wild animal in Central or South America is a better hunter than the jaguar.

A Jaguar Family

▲ *A jaguar cub*

Baby jaguars are called **cubs**. A mother jaguar may give birth to one to four cubs at one time. Cubs born to the same mother at the same time are called a **litter**.

It is the mother's job to raise the baby jaguars. Some jaguar fathers help the mothers take care of the cubs. Other fathers go off to live on their own.

The cubs and their mother live in a **den**. The den can be a cave in some rocks. Or it may be a hiding place in trees or thorny bushes.

▲ *A jaguar in front of its cave den*

▲ *A jaguar mother and her cub*

When the cubs are born, they cannot see. They are also very small. They weigh only about 1 1/2 to 2 pounds (0.7 to 0.9 kilogram).

By the time the cubs are six weeks old, they can see very well. They are as big as house cats. Soon the cubs are big enough to leave the den to hunt for food with their mother.

Young jaguars stay with their mother until they are about two years old. Then they go off to live and hunt by themselves. A jaguar is old enough to have cubs of its own when it is three years old. Jaguars live to be eleven to twenty years old.

Jaguar Tales

Long ago, native people in the lands where jaguars lived told many stories about this animal. These stories helped explain things that people did not understand. This type of story is called a **myth** or a legend.

In these legends, some animals had special powers. In the stories of the people of Mexico, Central America, and South America, jaguars had special powers.

Indians in the Amazon rain forest of South America believed that the sound of thunder was the roar of the jaguar. Another group of South American Indians believed that the jaguar was the god of darkness. A god is a superior being with great powers. Some native people of Central and South America believed that the jaguar's spots stood for the stars in the sky.

▲ *A Maya stone carving of a jaguar*

▲ *Images of jaguars are common in Maya art and buildings.*

▲ *Some ancient people believed the spots on the jaguar's coat represented the stars in the sky.*

In one old story, a jaguar swallows the sun. People used this story to explain the natural event called a **solar eclipse**. During a solar eclipse, the sun

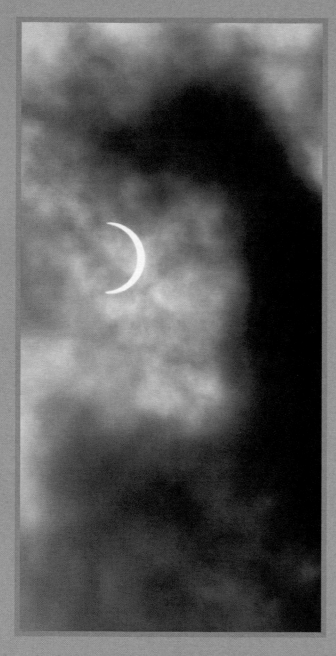

In the past, some people believed solar eclipses were caused by jaguars swallowing the sun.

seems to disappear. Today, people know that a solar eclipse occurs when the moon passes between the sun and Earth.

The Olmecs were an Indian people who lived in Mexico long ago. They believed in a god whose body was half human and half jaguar.

The Maya people of Mexico and Central America built a powerful empire. The rulers of this empire wanted to be as powerful as the jaguar. They wanted other people to think they were just as strong and brave as the animal. Sometimes, the rulers wore jaguar fur. They also added the word *jaguar* to their names. Two of the rulers were called Shield-Jaguar and Bird-Jaguar.

▲ *This ceramic urn shows a Maya man wearing a jaguar headdress.*

Jaguars in Danger

▲ *Jaguars used to live in the U.S. Southwest.*

Today, the jaguar is an endangered animal. An endangered animal is an animal that is in danger of dying

out. Today, there may be only 15,000 jaguars left in the world.

Jaguars are no longer found in many of the places where they once lived. There used to be wild jaguars living in Arizona, New Mexico, Texas, and other parts of the southwestern United States.

Also, fewer jaguars are found in Mexico, Central America, and South America. Their homes are being

▲ *As Central and South American rain forests disappear, so do jaguars.*

destroyed. The rain forests and grass-lands where these animals live are being cut down. People want to use the land to grow crops and build towns.

When the jaguar's home is destroyed, so are the homes of its prey. The animals that the jaguar hunts are forced to move out of these areas. Now, the jaguars must find other ani-mals to hunt.

Jaguars are strong

▲ *South Americans hunt jaguars to protect their farm animals.*

enough to kill horses and cattle. They may hunt farm animals and other animals living in the towns. To protect their animals, farmers kill the jaguars.

People in Central and South America eat some of the same animals that jaguars eat. When more people are eating wild pigs, fish, and deer, there is less food for the jaguars to eat.

In the past, many jaguars were killed for their beautiful fur.

▲ *Jaguars are sometimes hunted for their beautiful coats.*

▲ *The jaguar that left these tracks in the mud was able to escape hunters.*

At one time, about 18,000 jaguars were killed each year for their fur.

In some countries, it is now against the law to hunt jaguars. In other countries, however, people can still hunt these wonderful animals. As long as humans continue to hunt these wild cats, the jaguar will continue to be endangered.

Saving the Jaguar

▲ *A jaguar living in a zoo*

Scientists want to save the jaguar. They are trying to learn more about jaguars so that they will know how

to help these endangered animals.

It is very hard to study jaguars in their natural homes, however. Jaguars are shy animals. They run and hide when humans are nearby. So, scientists have to study the jaguars that live in zoos.

The best way to save jaguars is to stop destroying

▲ *The country of Belize protects its jaguars in a special park.*

the places where they live. If people stopped cutting down the rain forests and other regions where these animals live, they would help save this animal.

The country of Belize in Central America is a good example. Belize has set up a protected area for jaguars.

Maybe someday, other countries will create parks like these. Then, these beautiful and powerful wild cats will be able to live and roam safely.

Glossary

caimans—reptiles that look like alligators

coat—the fur of an animal

cubs—baby jaguars

den—the home that newborn jaguar cubs live in with their mother

litter—a group of jaguar cubs born to the same mother at the same time

myth—an old story that helps people understand the natural world

prey—the animals jaguars hunt for food

rodent—a small animal that nibbles, such as a squirrel or mouse

solar eclipse—the darkening of the sun when the moon passes between the sun and the earth

Did You Know?

- Scientists have discovered jaguar remains that date back as far as the Ice Age.

- Although people fear the jaguar, these powerful animals rarely attack humans.

- Ranchers hunt jaguars because, they say, the wild cats attack their cattle. In fact, studies show that jaguar attacks on cattle are rare.

- Jaguars climb trees to hunt for monkeys.

At a Glance

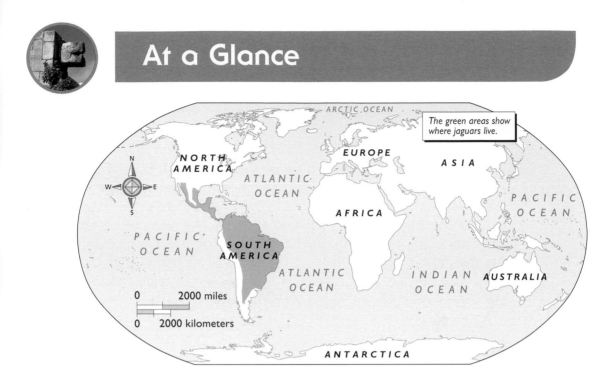

The green areas show where jaguars live.

Range: Jaguars live in parts of Mexico, Central America, and South America. They live in swamps, jungles, rain forests, and wooded areas.

Size: Male jaguars weigh 125 to 350 pounds (57 to 159 kilograms). Female jaguars weigh 100 to 200 pounds (45 to 90 kilograms). Jaguars are 4 to 6 feet (1.2 to 1.8 meters) long, not including their tails. Their shoulders are only about 2 feet (60 centimeters) above the ground.

Diet: Jaguars hunt more than eighty kinds of animals, including birds, turtles, monkeys, deer, and fish.

Young: Mother jaguars give birth to one to four cubs at one time. The cubs live with their mothers until they are two years old.

Want to Know More?

At the Library

Daddio, Monica. *Portrait of a Superstar: Humanizing the Jaguar.*
    Trenton, N.J.: Francella Publishing, 1998.
Smith, Roland. *Jaguar.* New York: Hyperion Books, 1997.
Watt, Melanie. *Jaguars.* Austin, Tex.: Raintree Steck-Vaughn, 1998.
Welsbacher, Anne. *Jaguars.* Edina, Minn.: Abdo Publishing, 1998.

On the Web
Big Cats Online
http://www.dialspace.dial.pipex.com/agarman/bco/ver4.htm
For information about wild cats and their natural habitats, conservation efforts, and many links to other sites of interest

Jaguar Species Survival Plan
http://www.aza.org/Programs/SSP/ssp.cfm?ssp=46
For facts about the jaguar and programs to help it survive

Through the Mail
Jaguar Conservation Project
Arizona Game and Fish Department
2221 West Greenway Road
Phoenix, AZ 85023-4399
To get facts and information about efforts to save jaguars living along the U.S.-Mexico border

On the Road
Exotic Feline Breeding Compound's Feline Conservation Center
HCR 1, Box 84
Rosamond, CA 93560
661/256-3793
To visit a wild cat zoo, with tigers, leopards, bobcats, and jaguars in natural settings

Index

About the Author

Darlene R. Stille is a science editor and writer. She has lived in Chicago, Illinois, all her life. When she was in high school, she fell in love with science. While attending college at the University of Illinois, she discovered that she also enjoyed writing. Today she feels fortunate to have a career that allows her to pursue both her interests. Darlene R. Stille has written more than thirty books for young people.